LEARNINGLINKS TO CHRISTMAS

TEACHER RESOURCES FOR THE RELIGION CLASSROOM

MAURICE RYAN

LUMINO PRESS
BRISBANE

First published in Australia in 2010

Lumino Press
PO Box 1024
Hamilton QLD 4007
Australia

Email: lumino@bigpond.com

Printed by Worldwide Online Printing - Hamilton
Typeset in Franklin Gothic Book 12/14.4

An entry for Catalogue-in-Publication data has been made in the National Library of Australia system.

Maurice Ryan, *LearningLinks to Christmas: Teacher Resources for the Religion Classroom*

ISBN 978-1-921538-07-0

The URLs contained in this book were checked for currency at the time of publication. Note, however, due to the dynamic nature of the internet the publisher cannot vouch for the ongoing currency of the URLs.

Other LearningLinks titles from Lumino Press:

LearningLinks to ... Jesus
          ... Mary
          ... The Gospels
          ... Mary MacKillop
          ... The Catholic Church in Australia
          ... The Sacraments of Initiation
          ... Prayer
          ... Story in Religious Education

Contents

Christmas: Teacher Background

The Christmas Story

The popular story and symbols associated with Christmas are based on a combination of details gleaned from the first two chapters of the gospels of Matthew and Luke. To these gospel accounts many traditions have been added by pious Christians over the centuries and from folk traditions of various European communities. When we study the Christmas story, then, we are encountering layers of narrative traditions from a multitude of sources developed over many centuries from widely different cultural groups. This complex construction of the Christmas narrative can lead to a confusion in the minds of students about the gospel foundations of the infancy stories and the meanings they contain.

This book focuses on the gospel traditions about the birth and early years of Jesus of Nazareth. Some consideration will be given to the way that traditions about Jesus' birth have been incorporated in Christian communities around the world. Materials and resources are provided that assist students to gain access to and understanding of the gospel texts and some of the historical knowledge that exists about the times and place where Jesus was born.

The first thing to note about the gospel accounts of Jesus' birth is that, of the four gospels, only Matthew and Luke mention the event. Mark and John report almost no information about Jesus' early life. A broad agreement exists among scripture scholars that the gospels of Matthew and Luke were written in the 70 or 80s CE, around forty to fifty years after the death of Jesus. The authors of these accounts are unlikely to have encountered any eye-witnesses of Jesus' birth and infancy.

In the first two chapters of Matthew and Luke, extended narratives of Jesus' birth and early life are recounted. But, the two accounts do not agree with each other on all details. In fact, only a few details are common to both accounts. Pious Christian tradition has harmonised the two gospel accounts into one, seamless story that has formed the basis for Christian celebrations of Christmas over the centuries.

We will consider, in turn, the story of Jesus' birth and infancy as it appears in the gospel of Matthew, then as it is represented in the gospel of Luke, and finally as it has been rendered in pious Christian tradition.

Matthew's Story of Jesus' Birth

Matthew's account of Jesus' birth and infancy begins with a genealogy - a list of ancestors - of Jesus starting with Abraham, through King David and down to Joseph, the husband of Mary (who is *not* identified in the genealogy as the father of Jesus). The names are large in number and often obscure in their significance for modern readers. The effect, however, is to incorporate the whole of the history of Israel into the story of Jesus. It signals to the reader that the understanding of Jesus' mission can be found by first reading the Hebrew bible.

The names in the genealogy are all biblical names, grouped into three sections each containing fourteen generations. Five women are mentioned, all of whom seem to have experienced some irregularity in their marriages. Each of these women exercised initiative and played decisive roles in the story of salvation of the people of Israel as recounted in the Hebrew bible.

In Matthew's story, Joseph and Mary live in Bethlehem. Mary becomes pregnant with Jesus without sexual intercourse with a human father. An angel appears in a dream to Joseph to direct him to take Mary as his wife. Matthew includes a fulfilment formula to link the events of Jesus' birth with predictions in the books of the Hebrew bible (Matthew 1:23). Jesus is born in Joseph's house in Bethlehem. The story implies that Bethlehem is the home of the couple - they have not come from somewhere else prior to the birth.

The magi (traditionally known as wise men) visit the house, following a star they had seen at home "in the east". In Jerusalem they had met King Herod. They bring three gifts of gold, frankincense and myrrh though no specific meaning is attached to these gifts in the story. Also, not disclosed in the story is the number of magi, always presumed to be three, in line with the number of gifts. The mode of transport used by the magi for their journey is not communicated in Matthew's story, though pious tradition has generally shown them mounted on camels.

An angel appears in a dream to Joseph informing him about the plans of King Herod to find the child and destroy him. Mary and Joseph flee with the baby to Egypt. In this episode, Matthew links the journey from Egypt with the story of liberation of the Hebrew slave people under the leadership of Moses.

Meanwhile, Herod slaughters all children in Bethlehem in an effort to destroy Mary's child. Scholars can find no historical evidence for this incident beyond the account in Matthew. When an angel once again appears to Joseph in a dream and announces the death of King Herod, the family returns to the district of Galilee. They make their home in the village of Nazareth.

Luke's Story

Luke's account of the infancy of Jesus is significantly different from Matthew's. Chapter one of Luke's gospel contains predictions and pronouncements about Jesus' birth by a range of characters. Luke's story is less structured than Matthew's. Luke stresses the parallel between John the Baptist and Jesus who are both acknowledged as agents in God's plan of salvation. But, John the Baptist is also a precursor of Jesus.

Mary and Joseph live in Nazareth, a village in the Galilee region. They travel from Nazareth to Bethlehem in the southern region of Judea, not far from Jerusalem. The reason for their journey is a census called by the Roman authorities. Luke draws attention to the fact that Bethlehem is King David's home town, who lived there when he was a shepherd. The images of flocks and shepherds will be significant in Luke's account. Joseph goes to Bethlehem to register for the census since this is his ancestral home. He is identified as a descendant of the royal family of David. Luke does not mention how he

thinks the couple travelled to Bethlehem, despite the donkey being a standard feature of pictorial representations of the journey.

When the couple arrives in Bethlehem, they find that accommodation in the town is heavily booked. They do not find any vacancies at lodgings in Bethlehem. But, Luke does not indicate where the couple go to stay while in Bethlehem. During their time in the town, Jesus is born. He is wrapped in swaddling cloths and placed in a manger, a feeding trough for animals of which there were two types, one wooden and transportable and the other a carved out hollow in the side of a wall. The existence of the manger therefore gives no reliable indication of Luke's ideas about the place of the birth.

Angels announce the birth of the child to shepherds in fields nearby who are watching their flocks. The shepherds find the child, recognising him in the manger. Eight days after the birth, the child is circumcised and named Jesus in accordance with what an angel had told Mary before the conception of the child. The child is then taken to nearby Jerusalem for presentation in the Temple in accordance with the law of Israel as outlined by Luke. Jesus is recognised as the messiah by Simeon and Anna. Then, Joseph, Mary and Jesus return home to Nazareth.

Christmas in Pious Christian Tradition

Because the two gospel accounts - Matthew and Luke - vary so much in their accounts, pious Christian tradition has dealt with the discrepancies in two main ways. One is by harmonising the two accounts into one seamless narrative; the other is by supplying details that account for gaps in the story or breaks in the logic of both narratives. In this section, we will consider some of these details that have entered the Christmas story after the time of the gospel authors.

The gospels provide no indication of the time or timing of Jesus' birth. We do not know from the gospels the time of year when Jesus was born, nor the time of day of the birth. Matthew ties Jesus' birth to the reign of King Herod the Great who died in the year 4 BCE. Luke mentions that the couple travelled to Bethlehem from Galilee for a census ordered by the Roman emperor Augustus. The only likely candidate for such a census was conducted around the years 6-7 CE. Estimations of the year of Jesus' birth are reasonable guesses, at best.

The situation is similar for the time of year and time of day. Despite the popularity of Christmas carols such as *Silent Night*, the gospels do not indicate the season or the time of day of the birth. The Roman festival of the sun god, *Sol Invictus* (The Unconquered Sun God), was celebrated at the time of the winter solstice in the northern hemisphere. As Christianity and Christian festivals took precedence in the Roman Empire, the celebration of the birth of Jesus replaced this pagan festival. The first year that December 25 was celebrated as the birth date of Jesus was most likely the year 336 CE, centuries after the event. This date then became the common one for Christian celebration of Jesus' birth, though this has never been universal among Christians. Many Christians who belonged to Eastern Christian Churches maintained the ancient practice of 6 January as the correct date.

There is no mention of a cave or stable in either gospel account of the birth but these are standard features in Christmas cards, Christmas carols and Hollywood movies. Matthew implies that Jesus was born in Joseph's house in Bethlehem. This is where the magi come to visit. (As an aside, if we follow the logic of the gospel narratives, the magi and the shepherds never encounter each other in the infancy narratives: Matthew introduces the magi and Luke the shepherds.)

In Christian tradition, the magi commonly have been represented as kings. In artworks they have been portrayed as riding camels wearing fine cloaks and golden crowns. As discussed above, they were always imagined to be three in number were and given names - Melchior, Gaspar and Balthasar. None of these details is mentioned in the gospel of Matthew where the magi are written

The Nativity, by Giotto di Bondone (c1267-1337). Fresco, Basilica of San Francesco, Assisi, Italy. Artists throughout the centuries have harmonised details from the gospels of Luke and Matthew as well as elements from popular culture to create a Christmas tradition at variance with the gospels.

about in chapter 2. In fact, very little information about the magi is communicated in Matthew, so Christian tradition has supplied most of the details. In Matthew's account, the magi represent the meeting of Gentiles with Jewish expectation of a messiah, a new universalism stemming from the history of the people of Israel.

Animals do not feature in the infancy narratives despite their constant presence in pious Christian accounts. The ox and the ass were a popular addition to the nativity scene among medieval Christians. The inclusion of these specific animals probably comes from the reference in the book of the prophet Isaiah 1:3: "The ox knows its owner, and the donkey its master's crib [manger]; but Israel does not know, my people do not understand." It is significant that Luke's story shows the shepherds, as representatives of the people of Israel, coming to recognise the messiah in the manger, a direct reference to Isaiah.

The focus on the nativity scene featuring the manger or crib in a stable is due to one man more than any other. At midnight mass on Christmas eve in 1223 in the small village of Greccio in what is today Italy, Francis of Assisi recreated a stable scene complete with crib and donkey. Francis was concerned that preaching and teaching about Jesus had become lacklustre. He wanted to revive interest in Jesus, and his dramatic tableaux about his birth began a tradition that continues down to the present day.

History or Sacred Story?

As historical documents, Matthew's and Luke's accounts of the birth and infancy of Jesus are of questionable value: they disagree with each other over essential details, they fail to provide significant information on key points, and they are not supported on essential points by the historical record. So, what value do they have if they cannot be trusted on important historical information?

Chronologically, the infancy narratives were later developments in the sources to which the gospel authors had access when composing their gospels. The early Christian communities took on elements of popular folklore, astrology and key texts in the Hebrew scriptures to help explain Jesus' origins. This was a normal strategy for creating literature about significant individuals in the ancient world, where access to reliable historical and genealogical records was limited. The intention was to assign a religious, political and cultural significance to the birth and earliest days of these significant people. The authors' intention was not to convey accurate historical fact and biographical information, at least in the terms that modern people would understand these qualities of literature.

However, as narratives of faith, the infancy narratives have a critical value. The meaning and significance in these accounts does not flow principally from their validity as historical records. Instead, the meaning is carried in their narrative power: these are lively stories, full of drama and tension that convey fundamental beliefs of the first Christians about Jesus and his life, death and resurrection. They are profound works of Christian literature, exploring the relationship between the followers of Jesus and the broader Jewish and Gentile worlds, the understanding of Jesus' mission, and themes that touch upon the most profound questions of life. They are the overtures to the main performances in Luke and Matthew. They introduce themes that will be played out throughout each gospel. They were written to invite faith in God among Christians.

Mary in the Infancy Narratives

Mary is the only adult mentioned in the infancy narratives who appears in the gospel accounts. However, her appearances in the New Testament's 27 books amounts to somewhere around 12 occasions only. We do not know as much as we would like about Mary from the bible. In the infancy accounts she is shown as compliant, a willing agent in the unfolding divine story of salvation. She is named as Jesus' mother in both Matthew and Luke, but her experiences are different in each story.

While we cannot be sure of the marriage experience of Mary and Joseph, the gospel accounts appear to confirm the knowledge historians have of the customs of marriage in ancient Israel. It seems customary that when a young woman reached puberty, she would be betrothed to a young man a few years older than her. The families would be involved in the process of ensuring that the pair were suitably matched. The girl who was betrothed - from around 12-13 years of age - would continue to live with her own family for around eighteen months when a marriage ritual would occur before witnesses and the young woman would live with her husband in her husband's family house. See Matthew 25:1-13 for some insights into the marriage process in ancient Israel.

During the time of the betrothal, prior to the marriage, the couple would live separately and would not engage in sexual intercourse. According to Matthew, Mary finds herself pregnant during this time of betrothal: "when Mary had been engaged to Joseph, but before they lived together" (Matthew 1:18). Because this situation would be the cause of some public shame, Joseph offers to dissolve the betrothal quietly, so as not to expose Mary to public ridicule. Divine intervention arrives in the form of an angel who advises Joseph against this course, explaining that this is all part of God's plan for the birth of the messiah (Matthew 1:18-25).

In Luke's story, an angel tells Mary about the pregnancy and God's plans for her and her child (Luke 1:26-38). In the unfolding story, Luke neglects to mention that Mary and Joseph become married after the period of betrothal, but this is an oversight. Luke certainly intends Mary and Joseph to be a married couple.

Joseph in the Infancy Narratives

We know surprisingly little about Joseph from the bible. Before reading on, consider the details the Christian tradition has provided about Joseph: he was the husband of Mary; a carpenter in the village of Nazareth; he travelled to Bethlehem with Mary for the birth of Jesus. Apart from these general details, the gospels are mostly silent about Joseph and his role in the life and ministry of Jesus. We do not know where he came from, where and when he died, what he thought about the Jesus movement, and how he spent his time (apart from being acknowledged in the gospels as a worker in stone and wood).

Christian tradition has supplied details to fill the gaps in Joseph's story. He has been rendered by Christians as a faithful husband, who may have had children from an earlier marriage. This is the main reason Joseph has been invariably portrayed as an older man in Christmas cards and Hollywood movies. If you look at most Christmas cards, you will see Joseph portrayed as an older man with a grey beard who features more as a older guardian of Mary than her husband.

The "children from a previous marriage" theory has been advanced to account for the mention of the brothers and sisters of Jesus. Mark's gospel mentions the brothers and sisters of Jesus in a text much disputed over the centuries (Mark 3:31-35; 6:1-6). Mark names these brothers as James, Joses, Judas, and Simon, though he leaves the sisters unnamed. One of these brothers, James, attained a prominent place in the early Jesus movement leading the community in Jerusalem after the death of his brother.

Since these texts challenge traditional Catholic beliefs about the perpetual virginity of Mary, the notion arose early in Christian history that these brothers and sisters were in fact the children of Joseph from an earlier marriage. (This theory was advanced by the author of a book called the *Protevangelium of James* which was written around the year 200 CE.) Another theory has been widely held that these siblings are actually cousins of Jesus: either children of Joseph's brother or Mary's sister. (This theory was promoted by Jerome, one of the fathers of the early Christian church.) This has been supported despite the fact that the author of Mark's gospel uses the ancient Greek words for brothers and sisters (*adelphos* and *adelphes*) and not the word for cousins (*anepsios*).

Joseph, because of his significance in the family of Jesus, will maintain a prominent position in the Christian tradition. But, the gospel accounts do not do justice to his prominence. Joseph does not make it alive out of the infancy narratives. He may have been dead by the time of Jesus' public ministry, a theory given some support by the fact that he is not mentioned in Mark's account of the family visit at Nazareth, referred to above.

Educational Responses

For religious educators who work with the infancy narrative texts with students, the additions and distortions of the pious Christian tradition present some educational dilemmas. Much of the pious tradition is at odds with the gospel accounts. The pious tradition created a narrative that was once described by Catholic biblical scholar, Raymond Brown as a "maudlin story". The pious tradition distorts the gospel accounts, shifting the emphases and interests of the gospel authors and creating images that owe more to European folk traditions, theological musings and the interests of commercial retailers than it does to the biblical texts.

So, when they teach the infancy narratives, religious educators offer a challenge to students' understanding of the birth beyond received cultural traditions. These traditions around the infancy serve to deflate the significance of the gospel texts as sacred stories that carry profound meanings for the Christian tradition. To be sure, this confrontation between sacred text and received cultural traditions can be upsetting for students (and their families) who may not have had the benefit of direct teaching of the gospel texts. They can see direct study of the gospel accounts as destroying their cherished notions of Christmas, and even of Mary, Joseph and Jesus - and much of the Christian tradition that they attach to this as well.

Religious educators need to approach these gospel texts with some care and educational wisdom. As historical records, the infancy narratives are almost worthless. They disagree with each other on key points, and there seems to be little historical material to validate significant public details. Students who wish to rely upon the gospel accounts for their historical content are preparing themselves for disappointment. Hanging on to dubious historical evidence for the birth of Jesus invites students, often in adulthood, to become sceptical of the nature of gospel literature and the claims of Christianity.

However, historical truth is not the only form of truth to which religious educators have access. The gospel texts can be approached as sacred stories that convey profound truths of the Christian tradition. We will now review briefly the sacred stories presented by Matthew and Luke.

Matthew and Luke's Sacred Stories

Matthew's sacred story of the birth of Jesus relies on a number of allusions to the Jewish tradition. Jesus is compared to Moses. Moses is described

Crib scene in the chapel at Greccio in Italy. Here, on Christmas Eve, 1223, St Francis of Assisi created a nativity scene and popularised a Christmas tradition that persists to the present.

in the book of Exodus as the leader of the Hebrew slave people who leads the people out of their indentured servitude under the Egyptian pharaoh to the promised land. In the gospel of Matthew, Jesus goes down into Egypt to avoid the Jewish king, Herod. Jesus is born in King David's home town. He will be the new David, leading his people. He will be the new Moses, leading the people on a journey of liberation, away from enslavement towards freedom and new life. The presence of the magi indicates that this Jewish king and liberator will be the leader of all people. Matthew's infancy story has a universal religious significance.

Luke also draws on the religious significance of Jesus being born in David's home town. Like the former shepherd who became king of a united Israel, Jesus will be the king of a united people. The significance of the birth is recognised by the shepherds who are able to see in the child in the manger the leader predicted by Isaiah. The child is born like another beloved Jewish king, Solomon who was similarly wrapped in swaddling cloths and nurtured with care (see Wisdom of Solomon 7:1-6). But this new Jewish king, Jesus of Nazareth, would be the leader of a reformed Jewish people. Luke's narrative attempts to position Jesus as the one foretold in the Hebrew bible and recognised by the shepherds. The child lying in the manger would be the king of the reformed and renewed Jewish people. Luke will tell the story in his gospel of Jesus as the prophet-messiah who will lead a revitalised Jewish people.

The religious significance contained in Matthew's and Luke's accounts of the infancy of Jesus is profound. The European folk traditions over the centuries have tended to trivialise these profound accounts. Modern religious educators have a responsibility to allow the texts to speak on their own terms unencumbered by pious traditions.

The Visitation by Giotto di Bondone (c1267-1337). Fresco on the wall of the Basilica of San Francesco in Assisi, Italy. The scene portrays the encounter of Mary of Nazareth with her kinswoman Elizabeth in the hills of Judea from the gospel of Luke 1:39-56.

Journey of the Magi, *T.S. Eliot*

"A cold coming we had of it,
Just the worst time of the year
For a journey, and such a long journey:
The ways deep and the weather sharp,
The very dead of winter."
And the camels galled, sore-footed, refractory,
Lying down in the melting snow.
There were times we regretted
The summer palaces on slopes, the terraces,
And the silken girls bringing sherbet.
Then the camel men cursing and grumbling
And running away, and wanting their liquor and women,
And the night-fires going out, and the lack of shelters,
And the cities hostile and the towns unfriendly
And the villages dirty, and charging high prices.
A hard time we had of it.
At the end we preferred to travel all night,
Sleeping in snatches,
With the voices singing in our ears, saying
That this was all folly.

Then at dawn we came down to a temperate valley,
Wet, below the snow line, smelling of vegetation;
With a running stream and a water-mill beating the darkness,
And three trees on the low sky,
And an old white horse galloped away in the meadow.
Then we came to a tavern with vine-leaves over the lintel,
Six hands at an open door dicing for pieces of silver,
And feet kicking the empty wine-skins.
But there was no information, and so we continued
And arrived at evening, not a moment too soon
Finding the place; it was (you may say) satisfactory.

All this was a long time ago, I remember,
And I would do it again, but set down
This set down
This: were we lead all that way for
Birth or Death? There was a Birth, certainly,
We had evidence and no doubt. I have seen birth and death,
But had thought they were different; this Birth was
Hard and bitter agony for us, like Death, our death.
We returned to our places, these Kingdoms,
But no longer at ease here, in the old dispensation,
With an alien people clutching their gods.
I should be glad of another death.

Christmas,   *John Betjeman*

The bells of waiting Advent ring,
The Tortoise stove is lit again
And lamp-oil light across the night
Has caught the streaks of winter rain
In many a stained-glass window sheen
From Crimson Lake to Hookers Green.

The holly in the windy hedge
And round the Manor House the yew
Will soon be stripped to deck the ledge,
The altar, font and arch and pew,
So that the villagers can say
'The church looks nice' on Christmas Day.

Provincial Public Houses blaze,
Corporation tramcars clang,
On lighted tenements I gaze,
Where paper decorations hang,
And bunting in the red Town Hall
Says 'Merry Christmas to you all'.

And London shops on Christmas Eve
Are strung with silver bells and flowers
As hurrying clerks the City leave
To pigeon-haunted classic towers,
And marbled clouds go scudding by
The many-steepled London sky.

And girls in slacks remember Dad,
And oafish louts remember Mum,
And sleepless children's hearts are glad.
And Christmas-morning bells say 'Come!'
Even to shining ones who dwell
Safe in the Dorchester Hotel.

And is it true,
This most tremendous tale of all,
Seen in a stained-glass window's hue,
A Baby in an ox's stall ?
The Maker of the stars and sea
Become a Child on earth for me ?

And is it true ? For if it is,
No loving fingers tying strings
Around those tissued fripperies,
The sweet and silly Christmas things,
Bath salts and inexpensive scent
And hideous tie so kindly meant,

No love that in a family dwells,
No carolling in frosty air,
Nor all the steeple-shaking bells
Can with this single Truth compare -
That God was man in Palestine
And lives today in Bread and Wine.

Write a Christmas Carol

Characters _____

Story line (with bible references) _____

_____

Setting _____ Time of day/ year _____

Theme _____

Story Board

Analyse a Christmas Card

This Christmas card has mixed together details from Luke and Matthew. The magi visit Jesus in a house in Bethlehem (Matthew 2:11). The manger belongs to Luke's account (Luke 2:7). No stable is mentioned in either account.

In Matthew, the star is said to indicate the house in Bethlehem where the child was, not a stable. The wise men enter the house, not a stable (Matthew 2:9).

In Luke, the child is said to be placed in a manger - a feeding trough for animals - but there is no indication of where the manger was placed. There is no mention of a stable in Luke or Matthew.

In Matthew's gospel, the wise men are not identified as crowned kings. Matthew does not say how many wise men visited Jesus. They do have three gifts - gold, frankincense and myrrh (Matthew 2:11).

Luke says the child is wrapped in swaddling cloths - bands of linen closely wrapped - not a flowing gown like this one (Luke 2:7).

Matthew's gospel does not say how the wise men travelled to Bethlehem. No camels are mentioned.

Alternative Endings

Write alternative endings for the stories in Matthew and Luke that tell about Jesus' birth and childhood. In each case, read the original story in the gospel, then write your own alternative ending.

1.
Matthew 2:1-12

The wise men did not return to their own country. They were worried that King Herod might find them, so instead they...

2.
Luke 2:1-7

Joseph is required to go from his home in Nazareth to Bethlehem to register for a census ordered by the Roman authorities. Instead, he decides to...

3.
Matthew 2:19-23

Mary and Joseph decided that they would not go to Nazareth in Galilee after their time in Egypt. They decided that they would...

4.
Luke 2:8-20

The shepherds hear from an angel about the birth of Jesus. But they do not go to look for the child in Bethlehem. Instead, they...

5.
Matthew 2:13-15

An angel appeared to Joseph in a dream and told him to take Mary and the child to Egypt. But Joseph ignored the advice of the angel and decided to...

6.
Luke 1:39-45

Mary was on her way to visit her relative, Elizabeth, in a small town in the Judean hills. But, along the way, something happened that meant she did not make it to her relative's house. This is what happened...

Infancy Narratives in Matthew and Luke

Matthew	Luke
Joseph and Mary originally live in a house in Bethlehem.	Joseph and Mary originally live in Nazareth.
	They come to Bethlehem because of a world-wide census ordered by the Romans.
The child is born at home to a virgin mother in the house.	The child is born to a virgin mother and laid in a manger.
	Angels reveal his birth to shepherds.
Wise men, bearing gifts, arrive following a star. In Jerusalem they had met Herod.	Shepherds visit the child.
The wise men thwart Herod's plan to find Jesus.	
	The child is circumcised and then taken to Jerusalem.
	Jesus is recognised as the messiah by Simeon and Anna.
Joseph and Mary flee with the child to Egypt.	
Herod slaughters children in Bethlehem.	
Joseph, Mary and Jesus return from Egypt.	
Joseph, Mary and Jesus settle in Nazareth because they fear Archelaus, son of Herod, who has become ruler of Judea.	Joseph and Mary return home to Nazareth.

Christmas Jeopardy

	Luke	Matthew	Christmas Traditions
100	They visit the baby Jesus	They visited the baby Jesus in the house in Bethlehem	This saint gave his name to the character of Santa Claus
200	The visitors find the baby lying in this	The visitors are guided to the house in Bethlehem by this	This is the date on which Christians celebrate the birth of Jesus
300	The visitors find out about Jesus' birth from these	The visitors bring these gifts	This name is given to the scene picturing Jesus' birth
400	Mary and Joseph travel from Nazareth to Bethlehem for this	This king looks for Jesus but cannot find him	Songs sung at Christmas are known as this
500	These two people recognise Jesus as the messiah	Mary, Joseph and Jesus go here to avoid the king	This soft drink company gave Father Christmas his red suit

ANSWERS

shepherds	wise men	Saint Nicholas
manger	star	25 December
angels	gold, frankincense, myrrh	Nativity, or crib scene
census	Herod	carols
Anna and Simeon	Egypt	Coca-Cola

RULES

1. The player selected to go first will select a category and a point value.
2. An answer will then be read from that selection.
3. The first player to respond correctly in the form of a question receives the points and chooses the next category and point value.
4. The teacher can create an answer for the Final Jeopardy question.

T-Chart

Question/Issue:

Response:

True or False?

Write True, False or Not Known to the following statements according to whether evidence exists in the bible.

1. Jesus was born in a house in Bethlehem.
2. Jesus was born in a stable in Bethlehem.
3. Three wise men from the East visited Jesus at his birth.
4. The wise men followed a star all the way to Bethlehem from their home in the East.
5. The wise men were kings in their home country.
6. An ox and a donkey were present at the birth of Jesus.
7. Joseph was an older man who had children from an earlier marriage when he was betrothed to Mary.
8. Jesus' manger belonged to the shepherds who were watching their flocks by night.
9. The gospels portray the innkeeper in Bethlehem as cold-hearted and unkind for turning away Joseph and Mary from his lodgings.
10. Jesus was born during the night on 25 December.

Answers

1. True. Matthew says that Jesus was born in a house in the town of Bethlehem (Matthew 2:11). He implies that this house belonged to Mary and Joseph.

2. Not known. Luke says that Jesus was placed in a manger (Luke 2:7, 2:12, 2:16), a feeding trough for animals, but some types were transportable and could have been placed anywhere. The non-transportable types could have been located in a cave, a stable or the downstairs room of a multi-storey house. Luke does not provide information on the type of manger or where it was located.

3. Not known. Matthew says that wise men, or magi, from the East who visited Jesus brought three gifts, gold, frankincense and myrrh (Matthew 2:11) but he omits to say how many magi there were.

4. False. Matthew says the magi saw the star rise when they were at home (Matthew 2:2). They then went to Jerusalem to seek information concerning the whereabouts of the newborn King of the Jews. They saw the star again when they were heading towards Bethlehem (Matthew 2:9).

5. Not known. Matthew offers scant detail about the background of the magi. Scholars presume they were astrologers and diviners. Christian tradition added details about the magi, perhaps relying on the words of Psalm 72:10-11: "May the kings of Sheba and Saba bring gifts: may all kings pay homage".

6. False. Neither an ox nor a donkey is mentioned in the Infancy Narratives. The reference to animals was added by Christian tradition probably based on Isaiah 1:3: "The ox knows its owner; and the donkey knows the manger of its lord; but Israel has not known me; my people has not understood me".

7. Not known. Christian tradition provided the idea that Joseph must have been an older man at the time of Jesus' birth in order to account for his absence in the Gospel accounts of Jesus' public ministry (which, according to this theory, must have occurred after Joseph's death). Another theory said that he may have been previously married with children to account for the identification of Jesus' "brothers and sisters" in Mark 3:31-35. No indication of Joseph's age or a previous marriage is given in the Gospels.

8. False. Luke does not say or imply who owned the manger.

9. False. Luke does not mention an innkeeper. He states only that there was no room for Mary and Joseph at the inn in Bethlehem (Luke 2:7), but he does not say how this information was obtained.

10 Not known. The Gospels do not indicate the time of day or the time of year when Jesus was born.

Time Order Chart

Write the topic in the centre square. Write events in the boxes and details on the branch lines.

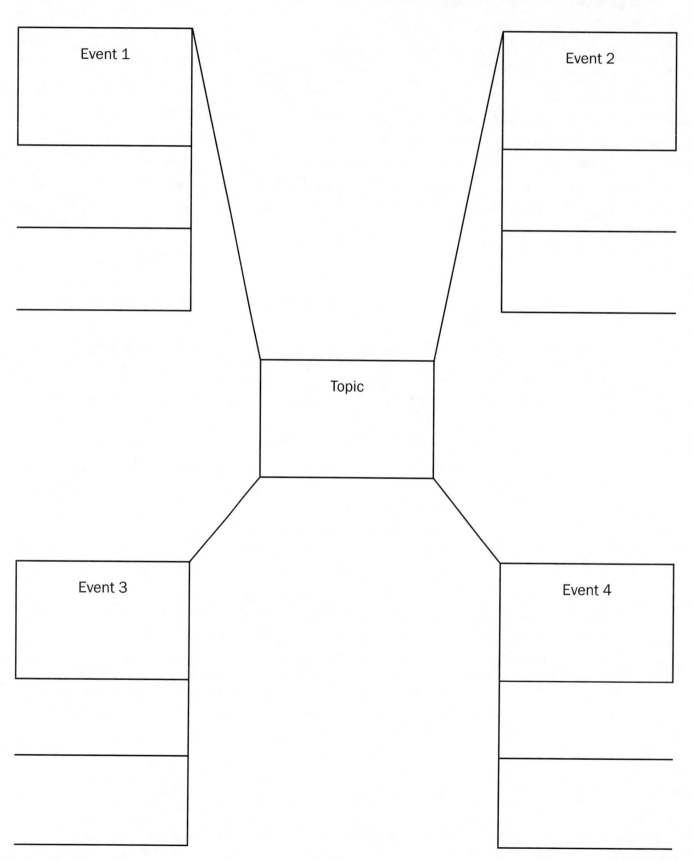

Event 1

Event 2

Topic

Event 3

Event 4

Research Christmas Traditions

Place	Customs	Internet	Notes
Italy	Crib scenes are placed in homes and churches.	www.whychristmas.com/customs/nativity.shtml	
Greece	A day of feasting and celebration, but not for gift-giving, which occurs at New Year.	www.gogreece.com/learn/christmas.htm	
Israel	Midnight Mass in Bethlehem on Christmas Eve. Celebrations in the Christian holy places throughout Israel.	www.thehistoryofchristmas.com/traditions/Israel.htm	
Australia	A big, Christmas dinner for family and friends.	www.the-north-pole.com/around/australia.html	
England	A Christmas tree stands in Trafalgar Square donated by the Norwegians to honour British support during World War II.	www.christmasrevelry.com/historical-christmas.php	
Christmas Tree	Decorating Christmas trees became a popular custom in the nineteenth century based on folk traditions from Germany.	www.christmasarchives.com/trees.html	
Saint Nicholas	Became the foundation for the story of Santa Claus. Archbishop in Asia Minor (now Turkey) who lived from 271-342. He loved children and helped poor people.	www.stnicholascenter.org	

Perspectives Grid

Read the story of the wise men visiting Jesus in Matthew 2:1-12. Use the Perspectives Grid to discuss how the characters in the story feel about each other. Write their thoughts, feelings and reactions in the boxes. You may need to imagine what their reactions might be if these are not clear in the story.

	Mary regards	King Herod regards	The wise men regard
The wise men as			
King Herod as			
Mary as			

The Shepherds Visit Jesus: Story Senses

Read the story of the shepherds who came to visit Jesus in Luke 2:8-20. Use the Story Senses worksheet to record what the shepherds could see, taste, touch, smell and hear in this scene.

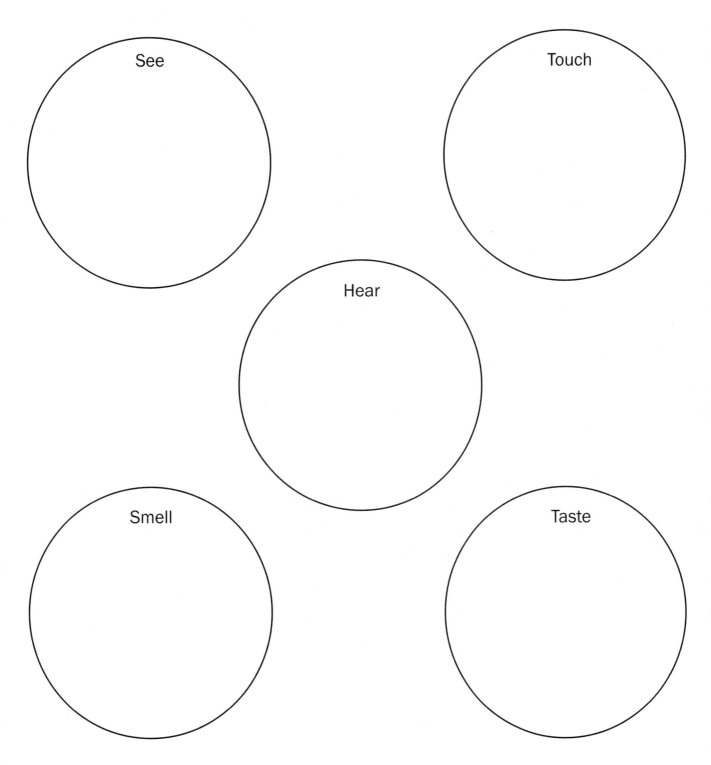

See

Touch

Hear

Smell

Taste

Activities for Early Years Students

1. Make nativity scenes using ordinary objects such as toothpicks, cutlery, twigs and sticks, pipe cleaners, or other materials that are easily obtainable and inexpensive. Students can recount the elements of the story they will create. Focus on one or other of the accounts in Matthew or Luke. Encourage students not to blend elements from the other story that do not appear in their chosen account.

2. Make a set of five sequence cards telling the story of the infancy from either Matthew or Luke. Discuss with students what is happening in each card. Then, ask them to place the five cards in the correct order according to the gospel account.

3. Collect a large number of Christmas cards that picture biblical scenes of the nativity of Jesus. Use these cards with students in various activities. Ask students to name the characters in the cards. Recount that character's part in the story of Jesus' infancy. Choose one card: tell the story of the card, creating incidents and dialogue - where do the wise men come from? what do they say to each other? Choose one card and act out the scene. Identify things pictured on the cards that are not part of the stories of Jesus' birth in the gospels. Group together cards that tell Matthew's story and those that tell Luke's. Make another pile of cards that blend the two stories or make up elements of their own.

4. Students can make a Christmas poster. Cut out pictures from Christmas cards or magazines. Glue these onto a large, sturdy cardboard sheet.

5. Use puppets to tell the story of Jesus' infancy. Invite students to tell their own version of the story using puppets. They can make their own puppets using a range of media: drawings of characters glued to sticks; hand puppets made from old socks; paper bag puppets filled with newsprint and faces drawn on the bag; marionette puppets made from styrofoam cups.....

6. Make up simple poems or rhymes about the infancy stories. Brainstorm key words from the story of Luke: shepherd, flock, manger, baby, swaddling cloths, Bethlehem, Mary....Students can make simple rhymes, make rhythms by clapping or stamping their feet. They can talk about the things they imagine as they tell their poems to the class.

7. Record students on tape or digital recorder as they tell the story of Jesus' infancy. Invite them to make a picture book to go with the tape. Classmates can use headphones to listen to the story as they turn the pages of the book.

8. Take digital photographs of Christmas celebrations and decorations. Display these photos in the class and discuss with students what they see in the photos.

Matthew and Luke Venn Diagram

Compare and contrast the accounts of Jesus' birth and infancy in the gospels of Matthew and Luke.
Use the Venn Diagram to record your findings.

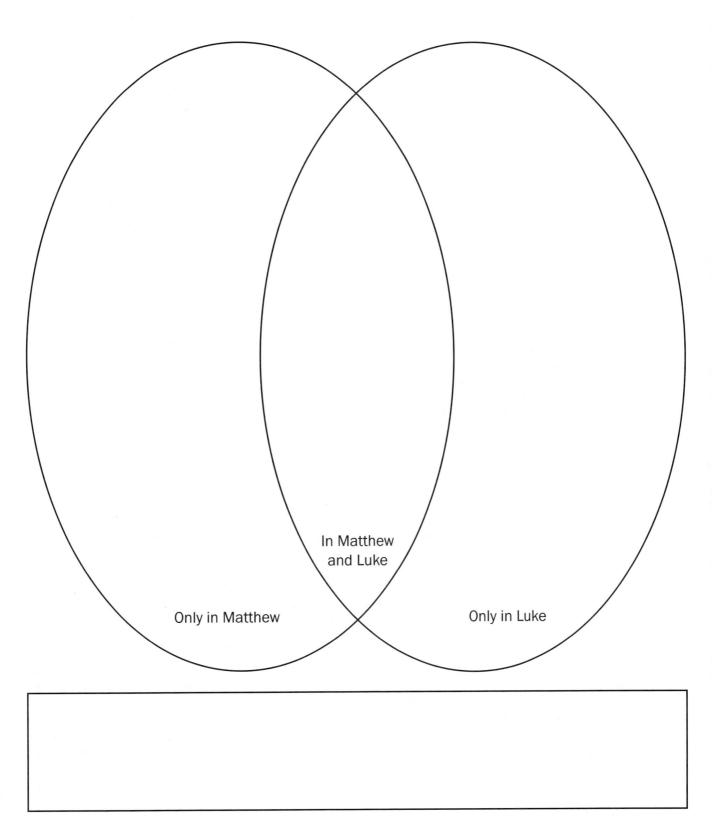

In Matthew
and Luke

Only in Matthew

Only in Luke

Birth Notices

Write a birth notice for Jesus that would appear in the *Bethlehem Times*. It is customary for friends and relatives of a new born child to place notices in the daily paper. Imagine that people connected with the story of Jesus would have placed birth notices. Consider the people listed below. Say what the main message of their notice would be. Then, select one or more of these people and write the full birth notice. Compile the selections into a class birth notice section of the *Bethlehem Times*.

King Herod   _____

shepherds   _____

wise men   _____

Mary and Joseph   _____

Elizabeth
(*Mary's relative*)   _____

Bethlehem villagers   _____

NOTES

In birth notices, the writer usually gives information about the circumstances of the birth (time, place), indications of the health and well-being of the mother and child, the personal meaning for the writer of the birth of the child and the relationship between the writer and the child. They may conclude their notice with a quote or personal message to the parents and child.

Stained Glass Window

Draw and Write

Title: _____

_____

_____

_____

_____

_____

_____

Analyse a Christmas Carol

Name of Carol	Details in Bible (*include bible reference*)	Details not in Bible	Notes

Carols

Silent Night

Ave Maria

Hark! The Herald Angels Sing

While Shepherds Watched

We Three Kings

Little Drummer Boy

God Rest Ye Merry Gentlemen

O Come All Ye Faithful

O Holy Night

Away in a Manger

The Holly and the Ivy

The First Noel

SCAMPER Christmas

Substitute	Who/what else instead?	What if Jesus was born in your home town?
Combine	Combine ideas, people, purposes..	What would the shepherds and wise men say to each other if they ever met?
Adapt	Adjust to suit a new situation?	What other aspects of the Christmas story might be emphasised today?
Modify	Alter, change meaning	What difference if Jesus was born in:
Magnify	Enlarge, add time, multiply	• a mansion
Minify	Make smaller, slower, less often	• a stable
		• a hospital
Put to other uses	New ways to use	What if the gold, frankincense and myrrh of the wise men were intended for: • Joseph? • Mary? • Jesus?
Eliminate	Eliminate or remove part or whole	What would happen is we only had the Infancy Narrative in the gospel of Luke, and not Matthew? (or vice versa?)
Reverse	Reverse roles	What would it be like if Christmas was not celebrated today?
Rearrange	Change order or adjust	What if Christmas was celebrated at a different time of the year?

Research Project - Life in Bethlehem

TASK

Research the life and times of Bethlehem during the time of Jesus' childhood. The gospels of Matthew and Luke say Bethlehem is where Jesus was born. Bethlehem was a small village when Jesus was born. It was a few kilometres to the south of the much larger city of Jerusalem. Find out about this area, what it was like, who the people were and how they lived at the time when Jesus was a child. You can choose the way you report your research. You can give class talk with Powerpoint, or you could create a mural with your classmates, or you could make a multimedia web page.

TOPICS

Choose one or more of the topics below as a focus for your research.

- Architecture (houses, public buildings/spaces...)
- Art (Dance, music, painting, sculpture...)
- Society and environment
- Religion
- Food
- Language and literature
- Political system
- Medicine

RESOURCES

Use the following resources to help you locate information for your research project.

- atlas/maps
- CD-ROM
- web sites
- artworks
- photographs
- videos
- museums (online)
- music
- encyclopedia
- books
- bible dictionary
- bible

Nazareth to Bethlehem

In the gospel of Luke, Mary and Joseph travelled from the village of Nazareth in Galilee to the village of Bethlehem just to the south of the city of Jerusalem in order to register for a census. Help them find their way to Bethlehem using the resources available on the internet.

RESOURCES

Many websites are available to help you. Start with these and use a search engine to find others:

- www.kidsource.com/kidsource/content/geog.html

- www.nationalgeographic.com/contents/

- www.mapquest.com

- www.goisrael.com

ACTIVITIES

1. Provide Mary and Joseph with a map for their journey. Use internet sites to help you create a map of their journey.

2. What is the climate like in that part of the world? What would it be like travelling in winter? in summer? When would be the best time of the year to travel? Why?

3. Where would the couple stay? What were the accommodation options available for a couple travelling then?

4. Write postcards back home from the couple to tell of their experiences as they travel. Use Postcard making software to help you design your card.

5. What money would they use to pay for their purchases? What would they need to spend money on while they were travelling? How much money would they need for their journey?

6. The couple would need to walk from Nazareth to Bethlehem. How far is the journey? How far could they walk each day? What is the landscape like where they travelled? How long would it take them to walk there?

7. Try to imagine what it would be like to travel with Mary and Joseph. Use your senses to describe your experiences: what would you hear, taste, touch, smell, and see?

Map of Israel

Use an atlas or resources available on the internet to label the map where Jesus was born and lived.

Bethlehem	Jordan River	Sea of Galilee
Jerusalem	Jericho	Dead Sea
Nazareth	Caesarea Maritima	Cana
Capernaum	Tiberias	Mediterranean Sea

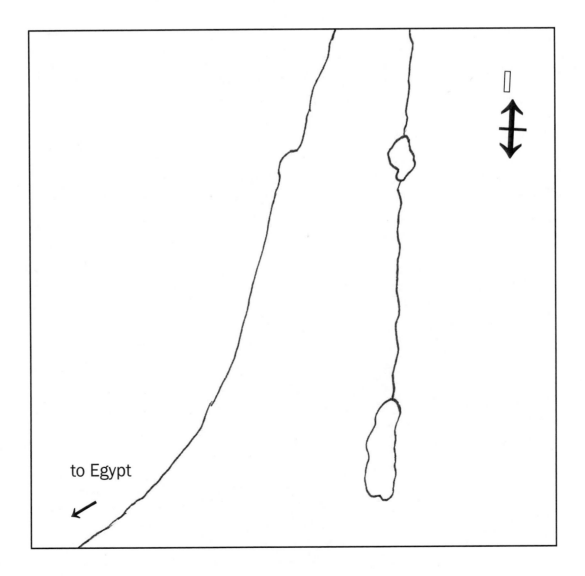

to Egypt

Analyse a Christmas Carol

The famous American carol *We Three Kings* was written in 1857 by Reverend John Henry Hopkins. He is reputed to have written the carol for the General Theological Seminary in New York City as part of their Christmas pageant. Read the story of the visit of the magi in Matthew 2:1-12. Compare Matthew's story with the carol below.

We Three Kings

How many wise men are mentioned in Matthew?

We three kings of Orient are
Bearing gifts we traverse afar
Field and fountain, moor and mountain
Following yonder star

What evidence does Matthew provide to establish that these men are kings in their home country?

O Star of wonder, star of night
Star with royal beauty bright
Westward leading, still proceeding
Guide us to thy Perfect Light

Where do the wise men come from in Matthew's story?

Do they actually follow the star to Jerusalem, or do they go to Jerusalem to ask about the star they had seen at its rising?

Born a King on Bethlehem's plain
Gold I bring to crown Him again
King forever, ceasing never
Over us all to rein

Frankincense to offer have I
Incense owns a Deity nigh
Pray'r and praising, all men raising
Worship Him, God most high

What does Matthew say the gifts mean?

Myrrh is mine, its bitter perfume
Breathes of life of gathering gloom
Sorrowing, sighing, bleeding, dying
Sealed in the stone-cold tomb

Glorious now behold Him arise
King and God and Sacrifice
Alleluia, Alleluia
Earth to heav'n replies

Do you think it is a problem that so many details in this carol are different from Matthew's story? Why, or why not?

If you were asked to bring this carol into line with Matthew's gospel, what would you change? Could you write a new carol based on this one?

Process Drama

Process Drama is a free-flowing dramatic activity that builds on but is not bound by the content of a story or historical event. It uses minimal props and staging. The teacher is involved in the drama as a leader of the action and provoker of responses as the drama unfolds under the teacher's direction. At the conclusion of the drama, students can be assigned tasks such as writing a report of their experiences maintaining their role as a journalist, soldier, shepherd and so on.

Life with the Shepherds

Students can be assigned the role of shepherd, watching their flocks of sheep and goats by night. Their humdrum existence can be enlivened by strange disturbances among the flock. In the dark, it can be difficult to make out what might be disturbing the herd. The shepherds can set out to determine what might be happening. The head shepherd (the teacher) leads the shepherds towards the village of Bethlehem quizzing the shepherds on what kind of a night they have been having? How has their routine been disturbed by the upset among the herd? What do they think might be the cause of the disturbance? As they travel look for clues: the dim lights from the village of Bethlehem in the near distance; the sounds of people calling out to each other in the night; the wind blowing along the gullies and hillsides. They can move towards these scenes, trying to find out what is going on in the village this night. Who do they meet? At the end of the drama, the shepherds can tell the stories of their interesting night in a speech to the whole group.

The Journey of the Wise Men

Imagine the students are a contingent of Herod's guard. Herod has just met with the wise men and has now sent out his soldiers to follow them to see where they have gone. Lead students on a journey from Jerusalem to Bethlehem, a distance of a few kilometres, in pursuit of the wise men. The teacher can assume the role of the head of the guard. Look for clues along the way - some gold, frankincense or myrrh accidentally left behind by the visitors on their journey. Ask the guards as they go why they think Herod is so keen to find the wise men? What might they do with them if and when they catch them? How many wise men are they looking for? How will they know it is them? At the end of the drama, students can write an official report to their commander outlining the results of their search.

Bethlehem Travel Agent

The teacher adopts the role of a travel agent in Bethlehem. Students can be assigned the role of travellers at the time of Jesus' birth. The travellers can be Jewish - from Galilee and other outlying districts in Judea - as well as international visitors from neighbouring countries. The travel agent must help the visitors to find accommodation in Bethlehem at a particularly busy time - a census called by Roman authorities. The travel agent takes the visitors on a tour of possible accommodation options in the town. They can visit an inn. Who runs the inn? What kind of people stay there? What is the accommodation like? They can move on to the houses of Jewish locals. Who is welcome to stay in the house of a local Jewish family? The travellers can go out into the fields outside town. Who stays here? What are the accommodations like? When the travellers return home, they can design a tourist brochure for people visiting Bethlehem in the time of Jesus.

Story Map

Title: _____

Setting:
Where?

When?

Major characters:

Minor characters:

Plot/Problem:

Event 1:

Event 2:

Event 3:

Outcome:

Comparison Chart

Use the Comparison Chart below to see how Matthew and Luke tell the story of the birth and infancy of Jesus. The answers to these questions can be found in the first two chapters of the gospels of Matthew and Luke. Write your answer in the correct box in the column under the name of Matthew or Luke. Give the bible reference for where you found the answer.

	Matthew	Luke
Where did Joseph and Mary live before the child was born - Nazareth or Bethlehem?		
Who gave the child the name, Jesus - Mary or Joseph?		
Who visited the child in Bethlehem - shepherds or wise men?		
Where did the visitors find the child - in a house or in a manger?		
Where does the family go after the visitors leave - Nazareth or Egypt?		

Cycle of Events

Title: _____

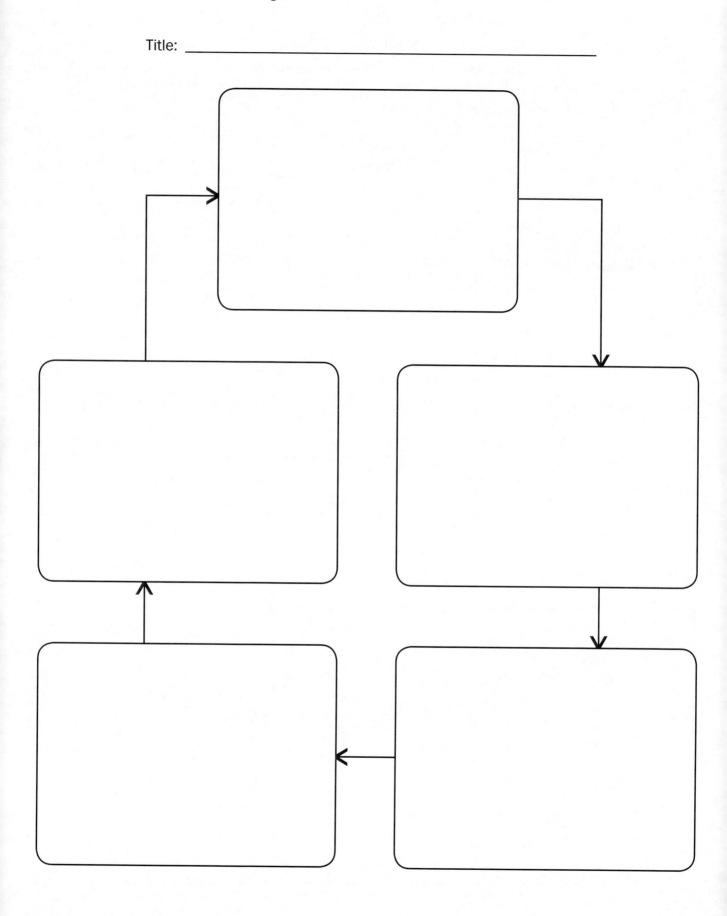

Christmas Celebrations

Read the story from Matthew's gospel (2:1-12) of the visit of the wise men to Jesus in Bethlehem. Complete the activities associated with this story. Create activities of your own based on this story.

Christmas Day

Describe what Christmas could be like if this was the only story of Jesus' birth we had. What traditions and customs might we have, or not have, if this was all we knew?

Christmas Letter

Imagine the wise men have returned to their homes. Write a letter from them to Mary and Joseph telling of their experiences after they left Bethlehem.

In the time of King Herod, after Jesus was born in Bethlehem of Judea, wise men from the East came to Jerusalem, asking, "Where is the child who has been born king of the Jews? For we observed his star at its rising, and have come to pay him homage." When King Herod heard this, he was frightened, and all Jerusalem with him; and calling together all the chief priests and scribes of the people, he inquired of them where the Messiah was to be born. They told him, "In Bethlehem of Judea; for so it has been written by the prophet:

'And you, Bethlehem, in the land of Judah,
Are by no means least among the rulers of Judah,
For from you shall come a ruler who is to shepherd my people Israel.' "

Then Herod secretly called for the wise men and learned from them the exact time when the star had appeared. Then he sent them to Bethlehem saying, "Go and search diligently for the child and when you have found him, bring me word so that I may also go and pay him homage." When they had heard the king, they set out; and there, ahead of them, went the star that they had seen at its rising, until it stopped over the place where the child was. When they saw that the star had stopped, they were overwhelmed with joy. On entering the house, they saw the child with Mary his mother; and they knelt down and paid him homage. Then, opening their treasure chests, they offered him gifts of gold, frankincense, and myrrh. And having been warned in a dream not to return to Herod, they left for their own country by another road.

Christmas Card

Design a Christmas card based only on the details in this story. Include a picture based on this scene, and words/greeting from this scene.

Christmas Carol

Compose a Christmas carol based on the story of the visit of the magi. Make sure to include only those details in your carol that are mentioned in the gospel story.

The Adoration of the Magi *by* Giotto

THE ARTIST

Giotto di Bondone (c.1267-1337) was an architect and painter from Florence, Italy. He was among the first to paint in the style of the artists of the Italian Renaissance. His life and career are shrouded in mystery. It is not certain when he was born or where he was buried when he died. Historians are not sure that all the great works attributed to Giotto, such as the frescoes on the walls of the Basilica of San Francesco in Assisi were actually painted by him. Neither can we be sure of where he learned his craft as a painter. Nonetheless, his works are among the most prized of the European art tradition. The *Adoration of the Magi* captures his interests in biblical themes and realistic depictions of human lives and emotions.

THE WORK

The *Adoration of the Magi* by Giotto is a fresco on the wall of the Scrovegni Chapel in Padua, Italy. A fresco is a painting on a plaster wall or ceiling. Many frescoes were painted during the Renaissance. Giotto painted this work sometime between 1303 and 1310. The Scrovegni Chapel contains many frescoes of gospel scenes, especially those which feature Mary. This work shows Giotto's ability to create images that were drawn accurately from life and to communicate deep emotion. His depiction of the human face distinguished Giotto from his contemporaries. His subjects' faces convey a range of emotions and responses to the situation in which they find themselves. Historians believe that Giotto was influenced in his depiction of the *Star of Bethlehem* in the painting by the appearance of Halley's Comet. In 1986, a space probe to the comet was named *Giotto*.

ACTIVITIES

1. See a full colour digital reproduction of this painting at www.giottodibondone.org

2. Find out more of the life and career of Giotto using resources on the web and in art books.

3. Describe what you see in this painting. What elements has the artist taken from the gospels? What elements are included from other sources?

4. This painting appears on the wall of a medieval church. What effect might this painting have on the people who came here to pray?

5. Download this image from the web. Make a Christmas greeting card using this image. Use card-making software available on the internet to help with your design and production.

6. Give your own opinion of this artwork. Do you like it? What do you think the artist was trying to communicate? Why do you think he wanted to convey this? Do you think he was successful in his aims?

7. Find works about the nativity by other artists from Giotto's time. Compare these works? What similarities and differences do you notice? Which do you prefer? Why?

Christmas - Multiple Intelligences

Interpersonal

Interview people on their understandings of Christmas

Conduct a small group research project on life in Bethlehem

Intrapersonal

Keep a diary as if you were a shepherd in Bethlehem

Make a list of favourite Christmas celebrations you have experienced

Verbal

Tell the story of Jesus' birth from the perspective of shepherds/magi/Herod

Debate: Christmas is more important than Easter

Logical

Compare and contrast Luke's account of the birth with Matthew's

Complete a story map of the events of Jesus' birth from Luke's gospel

Naturalistic

Investigate the flora and fauna of Galilee in Jesus' time

What were the seasons like when Jesus was a child in Galilee?

Musical

Compose a rap or rhyme on the birth of Jesus

Analyse Christmas carols for their biblical content

Bodily/Kinaesthetic

Create a drama on the visit of the magi

Prepare food eaten by Jewish people in Jesus' time

Visual/Spatial

Label a map showing the places significant to the birth of Jesus

Create a photo collage of Christmas traditions around the world

Silent Card Shuffle

star	magi	gold frankincense myrrh	house in Bethlehem
King Herod	shepherds	baby wrapped in swaddling cloths	manger
census	Joseph	Mary	Bethlehem
stable	ox	inn keeper	donkey

Duplicate the 16 cards. Place a set of 16 cards in envelopes, one for each small group. Each group simultaneously and in silence opens their envelope and spreads the cards on a table. In silence, each group arranges the cards into four categories: Matthew's account (star, magi, gold, fankincense and myrrh, King Herod), Luke's account (shepherds, baby wrapped in swaddling cloths, manger, census), both Matthew and Luke (Bethlehem, Joseph, Mary) and, Not in the Bible (stable, ox, inn keeper, donkey). The first team to sort their cards correctly into four categories is declared the winner.

Family Crest

Design a crest for Jesus' family. Include images and designs that communicate ideas such as the birth of the child, the family's religion, where they live, what their interests are, and so on.

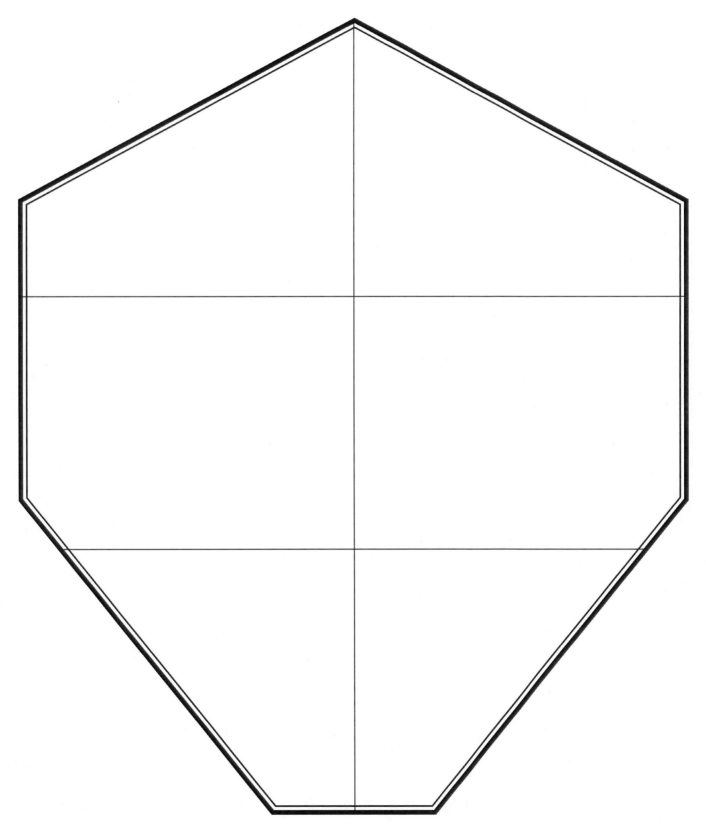

WANTED

KING HEROD THE GREAT IS LOOKING FOR THIS FAMILY

King Herod needs help to find this family. They were last seen in the Bethlehem area. They were seen talking to some strangers from the east.

Names of family members: Mary, _____ , _____

Place of residence: _____

Believed to be hiding in: _____

Why they are wanted: _____

King Herod, your kind and loving ruler, would like to meet with this family as soon as possible. He wants to help them with their young child. Read Matthew chapter 2 for clues to their location.

REWARD OFFERED! 50 SHEKELS

Flow Chart

Write the topic or name of the story in the top box. Then, list or draw the steps in time order.

Topic/Story:

Rank Order List

Use a ranking table to find out the most important characters in the stories of the birth and infancy of Jesus. Follow the steps in order to arrive at a list of characters in rank order, from most important to least important in the stories.

1. Brainstorm a list of characters who appear in the story of Jesus' birth. The list has been completed for you for this task.

2. The names of each character have been written down each side of the ranking table.

3. Compare each character in the left-hand column with each one listed across the top of the table. Write the name of your choice in each case.

4 Count up the number of times each character's name appears in the table. List the characters in rank order in the list at the bottom of the page.

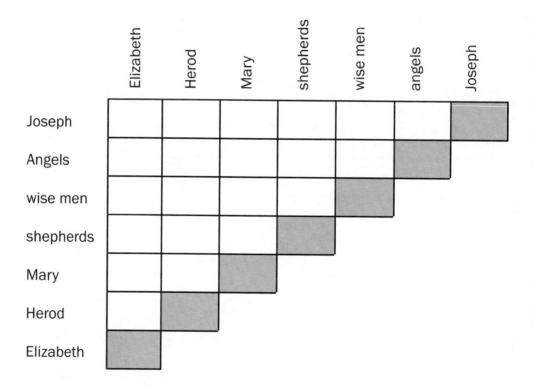

Who are the most important characters in the infancy narratives (in rank order).?

1. _____   5. _____

2. _____   6. _____

3. _____   7. _____

4. _____

Prayers

I Will Light Candles This Christmas

Candles of joy despite all sadness,
Candles of hope where despair keeps watch,
Candles of courage for fears ever present,
Candles of peace for tempest-tossed days,
Candles of graces to ease heavy burdens,
Candles of love to inspire all my living,
Candles that will burn all the year long.

HOWARD THURMAN

Christmas Prayer

Lord, in this holy season of prayer and song and laughter, we praise you for the great wonders you have sent us: for shining star and angel's song, for infant's cry in lowly manger. We praise you for the Word made flesh in a little Child. We behold his glory, and are bathed in its radiance.

Be with us as we sing the ironies of Christmas, the incomprehensible comprehended, the poetry made hard fact, the helpless Babe who cracks the world asunder. We kneel before you shepherds, innkeepers, wisemen. Help us to rise bigger than we are. Amen.

Christmas Prayer

When the song of the angels is stilled,
When the star in the sky is gone,
When the kings and princes are home,
When the shepherds are back with their flock,
The work of Christmas begins:
to find the lost,
to heal the broken
to feed the hungry
to release the prisoners
to rebuild the nations
to bring peace among brothers and sisters
to make music in the heart.

HOWARD THURMAN

Christ of a cold December,
quicken us to remember
poverty in a stable,
need, like the sting of snow.

Useful Websites

Jesus in Context
www.jesusarchive.com

This site contains a vast array of resources and links to other sites. Mostly for scholars and tertiary students, but will also be helpful as a source of background for teachers. The material presented is a summation of the best contemporary research and reflection on Jesus in the context of first century Palestine.

Biblical Resources
www.besthistorysites.net/AncientBiblical.html

This is another scholarly site, but more accessible for the general reader than the site listed above. The language and graphics are suitable as a teacher resource. Information is provided in bite-sized parcels and is issue-based, making it useful as a source of background information on specific questions such as Jesus' Jewish heritage and popular culture in Jesus' time.

Games Jesus Played
http://biblestudent.com

This site provides insights into the games played by children in the time of Jesus. It utilises gospel quotes and historical background. Brief, but useful. Students can research the game called "Mill" which was popular in antiquity. An outline for the Mill game can be found on the floor of the synagogue in Capernaum in Galilee, the home base for Jesus' public ministry.

Teaching Jesus
www.standards.dfes.gov.uk/schemes/religion

Classroom religion teachers are the intended audience for this site. It offers teaching and learning ideas on a broad range of topics. It includes a number of links to sites that focus on teaching Jesus to primary school students. Teachers will find many useful tips and ideas on this site.

Jesus and Food
www.members.tripod.com/~Barquentine/

This site is text only, but it offers a comprehensive survey of food in the bible. The discussion is clear, light-hearted and accessible. See especially chapter 17: "Was Jesus a Vegetarian?"

Jesus' Jewish Parents
www.jerusalemperspective.com/articles/DisplayArticle.asp?ID=1447

An informative and accessible article on the historical context of Luke's stories of Jesus' childhood and the Jewish rituals observed by his faithful Jewish parents. This site offers a strong foundation for a consideration of the Jewishness of Jesus and the circumstances of his birth within a Jewish community.

Bible Gateway
www.ntgateway.com

This is the address for the Bible Gateway site. It contains a large range of resources for studying the bible. Look for materials on this site for studying and understanding the infancy narratives. This site also contains a wide range of links to other related biblical sites. Extremely useful resource for teachers for any bible-related topic.

Silk Net
www.silk.net/RelEd/

Silk Net is a site created to provide Catholic religious educators with background materials and teaching and learning materials on a wide range of topics. The site has extensive treatment of topics focused on Jesus and the gospels.

The Birth of Jesus in Luke and Matthew
http://catholic-resources.org/Bible/Jesus-Birth.htm

A short, accessible and useful survey of the gospel evidence for the birth and infancy of Jesus. Helpful background for teachers and for senior secondary students pursuing research of this topic.

Jesus' Birth
www.religioustolerance.org/xmas_lib.htm

This site provides a lengthy discussion of the gospel traditions about the birth of Jesus and the likely historical and cultural contexts for these gospel accounts. A balanced and comprehensive discussion useful for teacher background and research by senior secondary students. It surveys many of the contentious issues involved in scholarship in this area.